CONTENTS

CAMBRIDGE UNIVERSITY PRESS
Cambridge
New York   New Rochelle
Melbourne   Sydney

INTRODUCTION

Cricket developed from a simple game of hitting an object with a piece of wood. However, by the middle of the sixteenth century, the playing of games was thought to interfere with work and lead to rowdy gatherings, so games were banned. Fortunately for us, not all of them died out, and cricket survived in country villages.

Its popularity grew in the eighteenth century because of the aristocracy's growing interest in it. They learned to play on their estates and liked to bet large sums of money on who would win a match. Since honour, as well as money, was often at stake when a match was played, proper laws of the game were needed so that disputes would not arise. The first recorded attempt to make laws was in 1744.

Clubs were set up in Kent, Hampshire, Surrey, Sussex and Middlesex. The Hambledon Club in Hampshire was the most famous. It was started in the 1760s by Robert Nyren, who was landlord of the Bat and Ball Inn on Broadpenny Down. His side was the best in England and beat nearly all others for many years.

New laws were written in 1774 and the Lord's Cricket Ground established in 1787. During the nineteenth century the game continued to gain in popularity, partly because of touring England sides who roamed the country and took on all comers. W.G. Grace was the outstanding figure of the late Victorian era. When he played, people flocked to see him. In the 30 years of his career he scored 54,896 runs and took 2,864 wickets. The most popular matches were those between Gentlemen and Players. The Gentlemen were amateurs, the Players were professional cricketers, employed by clubs.

Cricket also spread throughout the old British Empire and in 1859 the first touring side went abroad – rather strangely, to Canada and the USA. The first tour of Australia was in 1861, the first official Test Match between the two countries was 16 years later.

To begin with, Test Matches were played only between England, Australia and South Africa. The West Indies, New Zealand, India and Pakistan all joined the group between 1928 and 1947. The newest recruit, Sri Lanka, joined in 1982.

Cricket in Barbados; the batsman in this 'friendly' match is just avoiding a bouncer!

There have been a great number of changes in cricket in recent years. The 1960s saw a drop in the popularity of the game in several parts of the world. Something had to be done if clubs were to stay financially sound. Tradition had to be modified to suit business interests. This object was achieved by the introduction of 'limited-over' cricket and by the sponsorship of matches.

The popularity of the one-day competition soon led to it being introduced into international cricket. The limited-over World Cup competitions are immensely popular. Even night cricket, played under lights, in coloured dress with a white ball and black sight-screens is now common.

Today the MCC is the administrative centre of cricket, in control of the Laws and all changes and revisions to them. The Laws are standard all over the world and apply equally to the men's and women's game. They have stood the test of time over 200 years and the reason for this, in the view of the MCC, is that cricketers 'have traditionally been prepared to play in the spirit of the game, as well as in accordance with the Laws'. In cricket this 'spirit of the game' is of great importance; it means that players never cheat, never try to take an unfair advantage and always appreciate the achievements of opponents as well as team mates.

3

THE FIELD, THE GEAR AND THE CLOTHING

The field

Cricket may be played on a field of any size or shape. The grass should always be carefully mown and the boundary clearly marked with a line, flags, a rope or a fence. Umpires and captains are responsible for agreeing on the boundary before the game. It is important if there is an obstruction on the field, such as a tree, or a local custom relating to a short boundary, that they agree on it beforehand.

The pitch is the strip between the wickets. Its condition is always of great interest to players. Is it worn, damp or dry? If it is grass, it

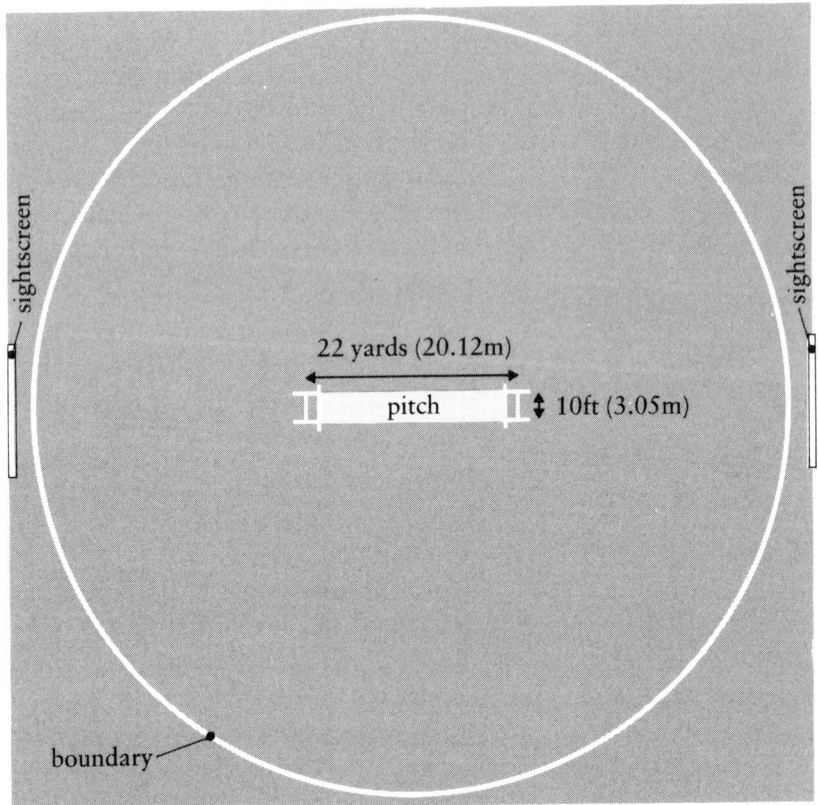

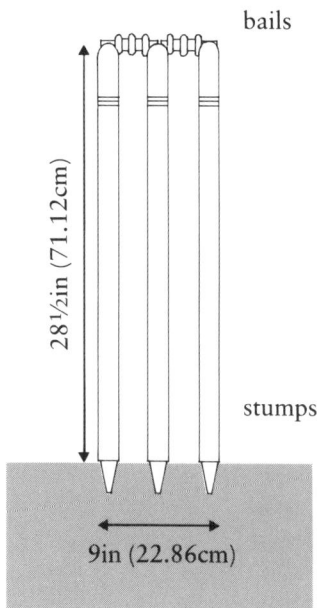

bails

28½in (71.12cm)

stumps

9in (22.86cm)

must be mown and rolled before the game, and for first-class games it must be covered during a match if it rains, to make sure that playing conditions are the same for each side.

The length of the pitch is 22 yards (20.12 m) from wicket to wicket. A shorter pitch of 21 or 20 yards (19.2 m or 18.3 m) may be used by boys and girls. The width of the pitch is 10 feet (3.05 m).

At each end of the pitch is the wicket, three wooden stumps placed in the ground in a line, with two wooden bails across the top. The wicket is 28½ inches (71.12 cm) high and 9 inches (22.86 cm) wide. The line on which the stumps are positioned is called the bowling crease.

Four feet (1.22 m) in front of the bowling crease is another line, the popping crease. These two lines are important for the batsman, because as long as he has some part of his bat or person grounded between them, he is safe. He is in his crease or ground. There are also return creases, within which the bowler must bowl.

Finally, you may notice, at either end of the field, two large white screens, usually on wheels. These sightscreens are to help the batsman see the ball as it is bowled. He may ask for them to be moved

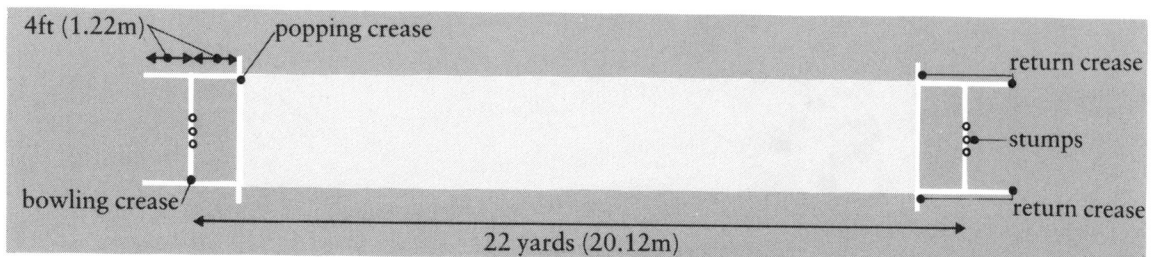

4ft (1.22m)

popping crease

return crease

bowling crease

stumps

return crease

22 yards (20.12m)

cap (or sun hat)

white or cream shirt
with white sweater

white padded leg guards

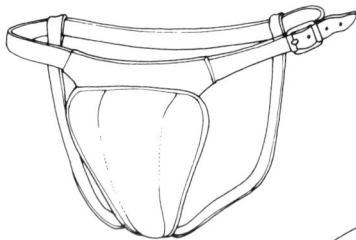

white flannel trousers

bat

ball

wicketkeeper's gloves

groin protector ('box')

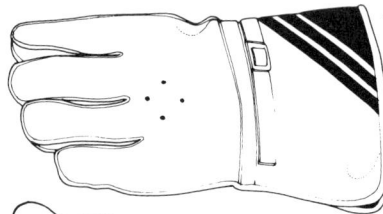

batsman's glove

cricket boots

so that the white background is behind the bowler's arm. Spectators should make sure they do not walk across them and disturb the batsman's view while play is in progress.

The gear

Bats are made of White Willow wood with handles of cane. On one famous occasion, Denis Lillee, the Australian bowler, came on to bat with one made of aluminium. He was sent off to change it. Bats made of new materials might completely change the nature of the game – as they have done, for example, in table tennis.

The front of the bat is flat and straight, the back has a bulge at the bottom. Bats may not be wider than 4½ inches (10.8 cm) nor longer than 38 inches (96.5 cm), but they can be of any weight. Your bat is a vital piece of equipment and should be selected to suit your height and weight. Boys and girls should choose smaller, lighter bats as a heavy bat may hinder the learning of strokes.

The ball is made of cork and twine, covered with red leather. It has a seam around its centre which is important in bowling. As the ball is used it loses its new shine and the seam wears down. Players rub or polish one side of the ball against their trousers. The shiny side then moves more quickly through the air than the rough side and this will help the ball to swing.

The clothing

Being well turned out for cricket can add to your confidence, so clothing is important. White or cream trousers, shirt, sleeveless or long-sleeved sweaters and white boots, are the usual attire. Girls wear a skirt or culottes.

First class batsmen facing fast bowling wear protective helmets. This is not necessary for young cricketers, but a cap or sun hat may be useful when it is sunny.

Batsmen and wicketkeepers wear protective pads on their legs, padded gloves to protect fingers and a special guard or box for the groin. It is becoming more popular for batsmen to wear rubber or crepe-soled shoes, rather than heavy studded boots, to improve running speed.

Bowlers should note that they are not allowed towelling wrist-bands, bandages or plasters on the hand delivering the ball (unless given special permission by the opposing captain). Wrist-watches may reflect a flash of light which could distract a batsman, so they are removed for cricket.

PLAYING THE GAME

Names of positions for the fielding team

A cricket match is played between two sides of eleven players, one of whom in each side is the captain. The object is to score more runs

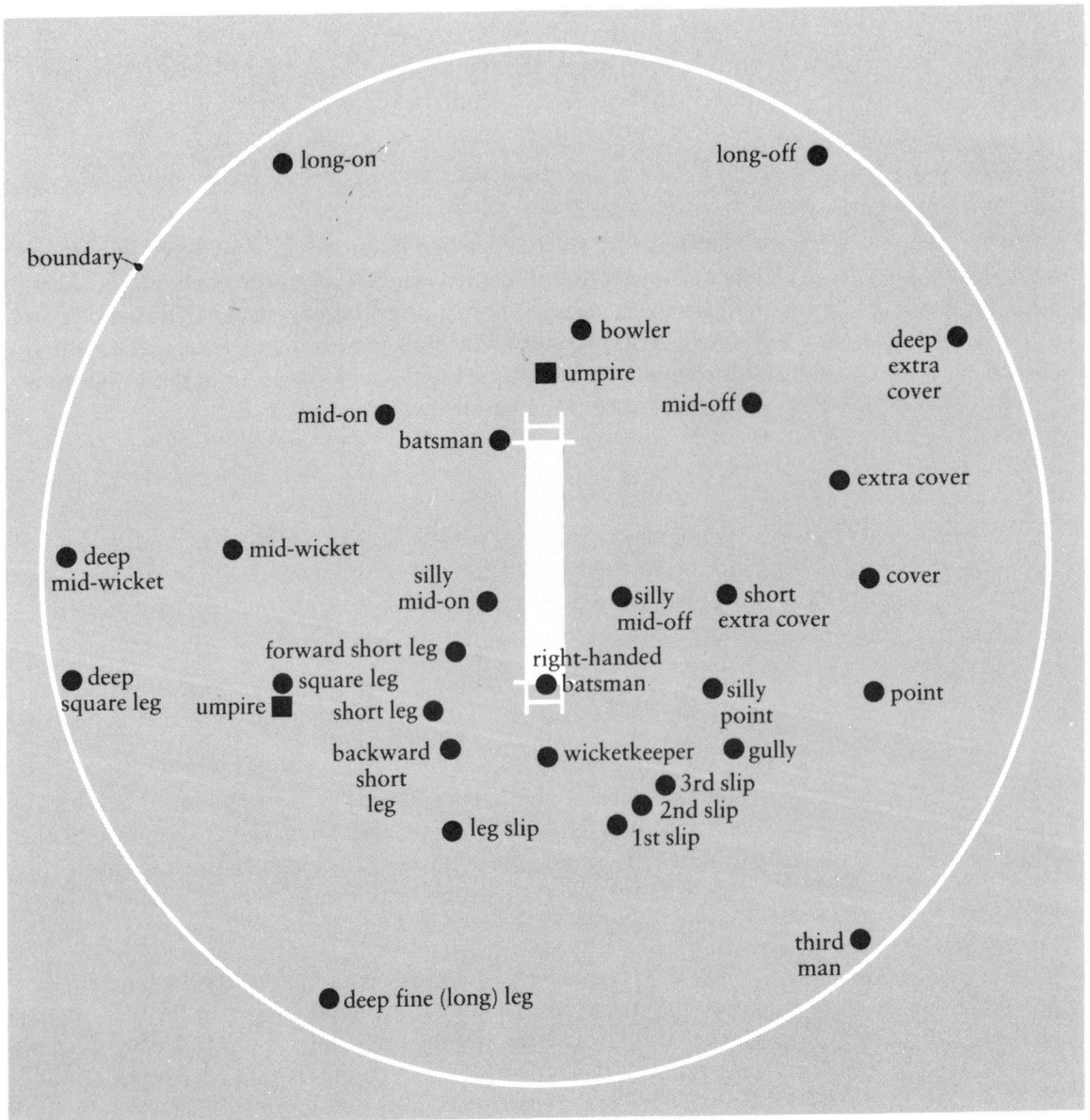

long-on

long-off

boundary

bowler

umpire

deep extra cover

mid-on

mid-off

batsman

extra cover

deep mid-wicket

mid-wicket

cover

silly mid-on

silly mid-off

short extra cover

forward short leg

deep square leg

square leg

umpire

short leg

right-handed batsman

silly point

point

backward short leg

wicketkeeper

gully

3rd slip

2nd slip

leg slip

1st slip

third man

deep fine (long) leg

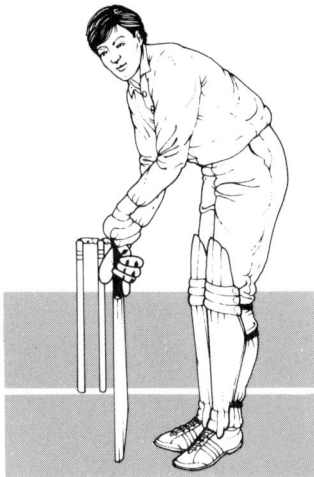

leg stump
('one-leg')

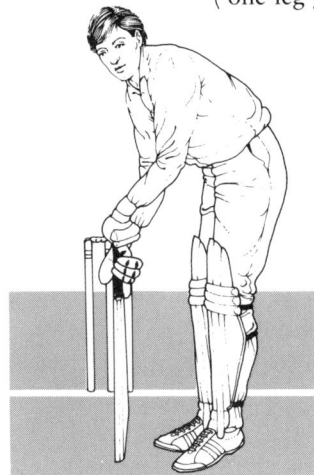

middle and leg stump
('two-leg')

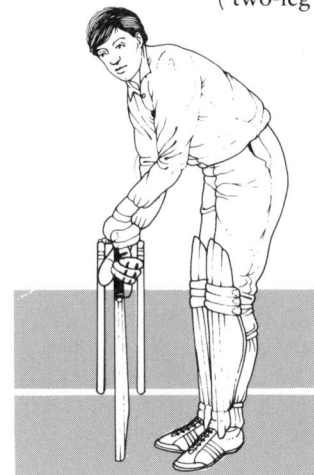

middle stump
('centre')

than the other side, and each side has a chance to score runs in turn. These turns are called innings. Matches may be of one or two innings for each side – and this is always decided beforehand.

Before the start of the match, the captain nominates his eleven players. There may be a 12th man who can substitute for a fielder or run for an injured batsman during a match, but he may not bat or bowl for another player. The captain draws up a batting order and tells his players their batting position. The best batsmen usually go in to bat early on.

The start of a match is decided by the toss. The captains go on to the field and toss a coin. The home captain tosses and the visitor calls. The winner decides whether his side or his opponents will bat first. This decision is based on careful consideration of the condition of the pitch, the weather, the type of match and the opponents. Once the decision has been made, all the non-batting or fielding side prepare to come onto the field and the opening batsmen of the batting side 'pad up' to take the field.

The two umpires are the first to come out onto the field. They check that the wickets are straight and the bails are in position, then take up their positions as the fielding side come out. One of the umpires will take with him the ball to be used. This will, usually, be a new ball.

The two batsmen are the last to come out onto the field. They take up positions, one at each wicket. The batsman about to receive the first ball is the striker.

The area of the field to the right of the batsman (if he is right-handed) is known as his off side and the stump furthest away, the off stump. The area to the left is called the on or leg side and the stump to his left, nearest his legs, the leg stump. The field and stumps are named in relation to the striking batsman.

When you come in to bat you 'take your guard'. The position you take up in front of your wicket is to defend the stumps. Each new batsman takes his guard before he plays by holding the bat straight, with its bottom or 'toe' on the popping crease and asking the umpire to direct him to the guard he asks for. This may be lined up with middle stump (when he asks for 'middle' or 'centre'), leg stump ('one leg'), or covering the two at middle and leg ('two leg').

Meanwhile, the captain of the fielding side chooses his first bowler. Each bowler will bowl six balls from one end of the pitch to the striker at the other end. Then another bowler will bowl six balls from the other end. Each set of balls is called an over. A bowler may

9

bowl the overs from one end for a period and this is known as a spell of bowling. He may also switch ends but he cannot bowl two overs in succession.

The captain and the bowler together place the fielders in position. One of them will be padded up and he is the wicketkeeper and will always be in position behind the stumps of the striker. The other nine fielders will be carefully placed according to the type of bowler, the tactics of the side and whether the batsman is right- or left-handed. After each over the fielders change positions for the bowler from the other end.

There are only two restrictions on where fielders may be placed. Until the ball is played by the striker (or he has missed it) no fielder is allowed to stand on the pitch, lean over it or cast a shadow onto it; nor can there be more than two fielders behind the popping crease on the leg side. The captain may choose an attacking sort of field, aimed at getting batsmen out, or a defensive field aimed at keeping down the number of runs made.

So umpires and fielders are in position, bowler ready at the end of his run-up, the striking batsman looks around at the field to

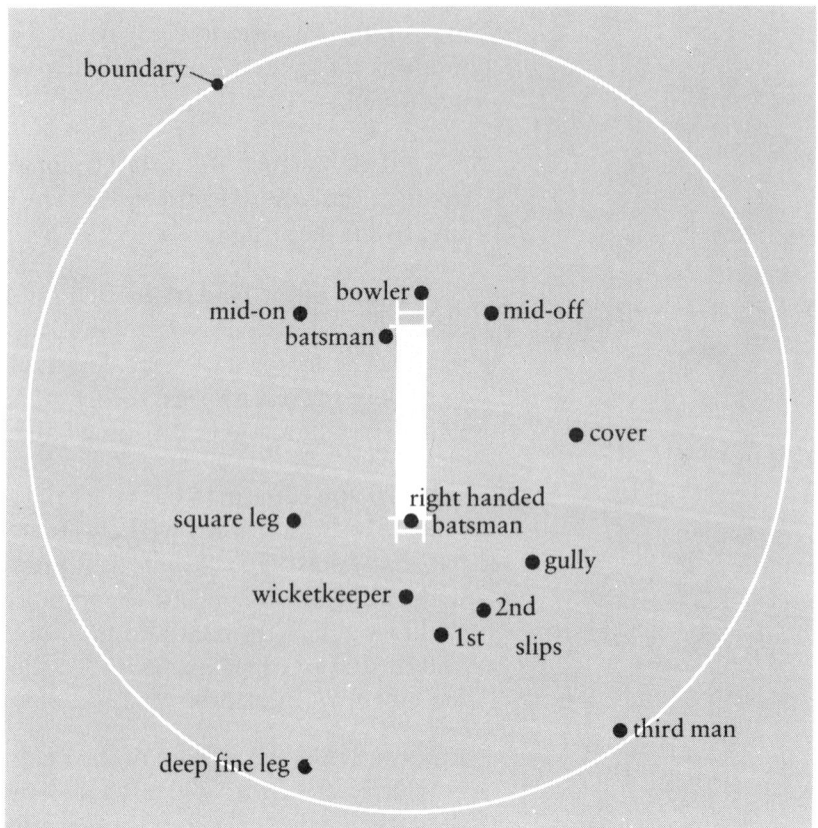

A typical 'field' with a medium-fast bowler

David Constant with a light meter checking the light before a first-class match begins ... and a lively spectator ready for play on his village green

memorise it, and when the umpire sees he is ready he calls 'play' and the game begins.

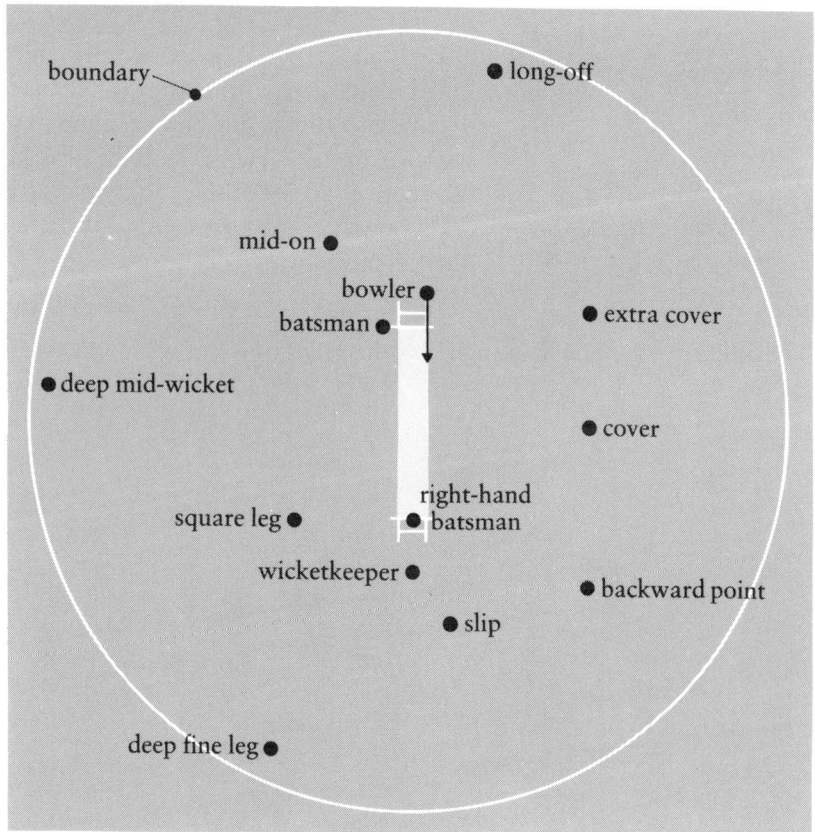

A typical 'field' with a slow off-spin bowler

SCORING RUNS

The object of your team when you are the batting side is to score runs, and there are three ways of doing this:
- by hitting the ball and running
- by hitting the ball to the boundary or over it
- from extras arising from penalties to the bowler and from byes.

Hitting the ball

Each batsman has a chance to score runs when it is his turn to face the bowler. When the striker hits a ball, the two batsmen may run if they choose. They do not have to run, but if the run is to be scored both batsmen must run, because it does not count until they have crossed, changed ends and reached the other crease.

Only the striker can score a run, but since either of the batsmen may be out at any time, they must share the responsibility for deciding to run and deciding when to stop. Generally, the batsman with the better view of the path of the ball takes charge and calls instructions to the other. Judgement of runs is a vital part of the game and you will not be very popular with your team if you get your partners run out!

The umpire will signal 'one-short' for this; the bat is not behind the crease

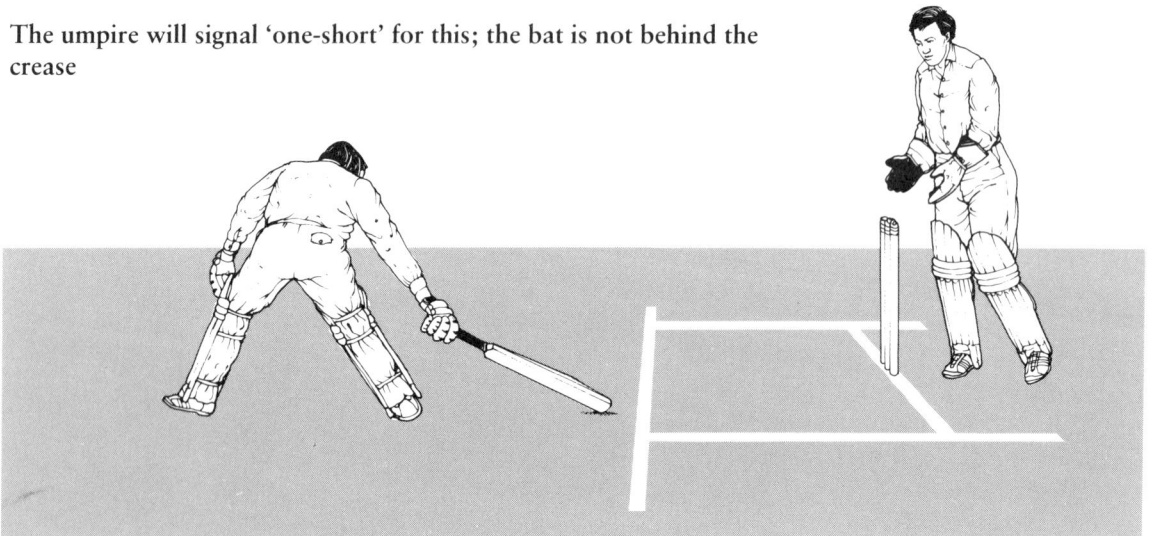

A contrast in styles between English cricket stars. Rachel Heyhoe-Flint demonstrates a perfect off-drive while Ian Botham shows unorthodox style in achieving the same result

It is necessary to touch the ground between the crease line and the stumps with a bat or foot, before turning and running again. The umpire will be watching, and should either of the batsmen fail to make good his ground in turning for another run, the umpire will signal a 'short run'. This run will not count, but batsmen do not return and complete the uncompleted run. Once they have crossed they must always continue to the other wicket.

Boundaries

The batsmen may run as many times as they can before the ball is returned to the wicket, but if the ball reaches the boundary of the field, it automatically counts as four runs. Then they can stop running and return to the crease they occupied when the shot was played.

If the ball flies right over the boundary mark without touching the ground first, it counts as six runs. A fielder who touches the ball or catches the ball and tumbles over the boundary with it, will not alter this. It still counts as six runs.

Overthrows

Sometimes a fielder makes a wild return throw to the wicket and the ball goes shooting off in another direction. This is a chance not to be missed! The batsmen may run again and score more runs. The striker may even score four additional runs if the ball gets to the boundary. These overthrows are added to the runs already made by the striker at the time of the bad throw. The run in progress counts if the batsmen have crossed.

Fielders can stop the ball with any part of their body. But, if they were to use anything else, such as a cap, five runs would be given to the batsman as a penalty to the fielder.

In fact the batsmen can run as long as the ball is in play. This begins when the bowler has the ball and starts his run-up and ends when the ball is in the hands of the wicketkeeper at one end or the bowler at the other end of the pitch, or when the ball crosses the boundary or a batsman is out. Then the ball is considered dead. On rare occasions 'dead ball' may be signalled by the umpire if the ball lodges in the clothing of a batsman, or the umpire.

Runs, boundaries and overthrows are all credited to the score of the batsman who is striker. Other runs, known as extras, fall into three categories – no balls, wides and byes.

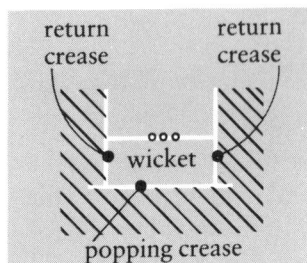

No balls

The 'no ball' is a way of giving the bowler a penalty if he has not bowled according to the rules. It is nearly always the result of a foot fault.

return crease   return crease

○○○
wicket

popping crease

(a)

At the point of delivery of the ball the bowler's front foot must not land beyond the popping crease in this area (as it does in (a))

(b)

Nor must his back foot land in this area beside the return crease (as it does in (b))

The rule is that the bowler must have his back foot inside and not touching the return crease and at least some part of his front foot behind the popping crease, as he delivers the ball. The diagrams make this clear, and it looks quite simple; but remember that when the bowler runs in to bowl, he will be watching the striker's wicket and will not have his eye on the crease. If his run-up is not just right, the front foot may go over the line.

For the batsman, the no ball is a bonus. If he does not play a stroke at all, one run is added as an extra to the total. In addition, the bowler must bowl another delivery in the over to replace the no ball. However, when the batsman hears the call 'no ball' he may well decide to try his luck and hit the ball. If he makes a mistake he is not out anyway. Even if he hits the ball and does not run, the one run is scored as an extra. But if he hits the ball and runs, the runs will appear on his own total. Remember that either batsman can still be run out in the usual way from a no ball.

A 'no ball' call will also result from any unfair ball: for example, a change in the style of bowling that takes place without the umpire being informed, or if the bowler throws the ball at the striker's wicket before bowling, in an attempt to run him out.

Wide ball

It is only fair that the bowler should bowl balls that the batsman is capable of reaching from his normal position at the wicket. If a ball is too high or so wide that the umpire thinks it could not have

A wide

been hit, he will signal a 'wide'. One extra will be scored on the total and another ball will be bowled in the over.

Obviously, if the batsman hits a very wide delivery, the umpire cannot call 'wide'. Because of this, wides can never be credited to a striker's own score. Any runs made from misfields from wides are always counted as extras.

Bye and leg bye

Byes, if the batsman misses the ball but manages to score runs

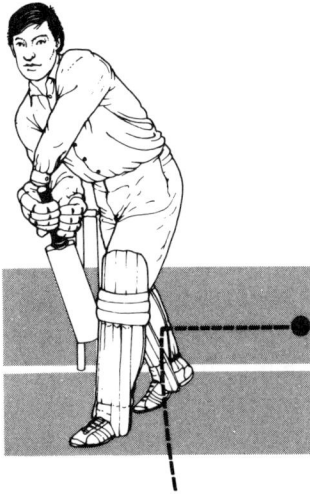

A leg-bye

The last sort of extras are 'byes'. If a ball is a fair delivery and goes past the striker without touching his bat or his body, and the batsmen score runs, they are put down as byes. The bowler does not bowl an additional ball.

Leg byes are also runs made from a fair delivery which the batsman has not hit with his bat, but which has touched some part of the body of the batsman. If the batsman has been hit by the ball as he tried to play a shot and missed, or tried to duck or move to avoid being hit by the ball itself, he may run leg byes and score extras from them. (Remember, your hands count as part of the bat – runs, not leg byes, will be scored off your gloves.)

A batsman is not allowed to score runs from leg byes by using his body to get the ball away, on purpose. This is cricket, not football! If he tries to, he will be called back by the umpire and the runs will not be allowed.

GETTING OUT

When it's your turn to bat, imagine that you are guarding your wicket and your only weapon is your bat. The fielding side are all trying to get you out, but it is up to the umpire alone to make the decision. The fielding side have to ask the umpire and will call 'How's that?' when they think they have got you out. Unless the fielders appeal to the umpire in this way, he cannot give you out.

There are eleven different ways of being out that may be recorded in the score book. The most common ones are:
- bowled
- hit wicket
- caught
- lbw (leg before wicket)
- stumped
- run out.

Three others are less usual and result from unlawful play by the batsman; you should be able to make sure they never appear against your name. These are:
- hit ball twice
- handled ball
- obstructing a fielder.

The words 'timed out' will appear in the book if a batsman has failed to come in to bat within the allotted time. Finally, you may have to retire hurt, or choose to close your innings.

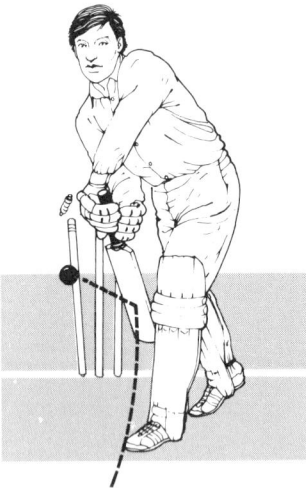

Bowled

When a fair delivery is bowled at you and it breaks your wicket, you are out as long as at least one of the bails is dislodged. Even if the ball has touched you first, or bounced off some part of your body or bat, if it travels on to break the wicket you are bowled and the bowler will claim the wicket with great delight.

'Played on' is the term used to describe when you hit the ball on to your own wicket, but it still goes in the book as 'bowled'.

Hit wicket

Not only the ball can break the wicket. If, while you are playing a

Played-on

Hit wicket

Out

shot, you hit your own wicket with your bat, your body or your clothing, you will be out.

It pays to be sure you know exactly how far back your wicket is when you start your backswing or indeed when you follow through on shots such as the hook. If you stumble and fall on the wicket while dodging a delivery, or even if your cap falls off and dislodges a bail, it will count and the bowler will claim the wicket.

However, you won't be out for hitting your wicket when you are running to it to get back into your ground and avoid being run out, or if you have to dodge to avoid a ball being thrown back to the wicket by a fielder.

Caught

You will be out 'caught' if you hit the ball with your bat (and that includes your hands) and it is caught by a fielder before it touches the ground. A fielder on the boundary must have both of his feet inside the boundary line when he catches the ball. If he steps over the line or tumbles over as he makes the catch or even just after he has caught the ball, it will count as six runs for you.

It will still be a fair catch even if the ball has touched an umpire, another fielder or another batsman; incredible juggling acts sometimes take place between the slip fielders. However, a fair catch can't be made off a fielder's helmet.

If the bowler catches the ball himself, it is known as 'caught and bowled'. The wicketkeeper is often in a good position to take catches from balls that are just nicked by the striker. This can create difficult decisions for the umpire, who must decide whether or not the ball came off the bat.

Leg before wicket (lbw)

The idea behind the lbw law is very simple. Your wicket must be guarded by your bat and this law is to stop you from using your leg pads to defend your wicket. The reason why it is sometimes a controversial way of getting out, is because it relies on the opinion of the umpire. Fortunately, whatever the batsman or fielders feel, the umpire has the final say.

You can only be out 'lbw' to a fair ball that has not touched your bat or your hands on the bat before it hits your pads.

If you play a shot and miss and it hits you, your equipment or your clothing, the umpire will have to decide, if asked by the fielding side, if the ball would have hit the wicket, had it not been stopped by you.

The umpire must ask himself these questions:
- Did the ball pitch (or bounce) in a straight line between the stumps at either end, or just outside the off stump?
- Was the point of impact in a straight line between wicket and wicket?
- Would the ball have hit the wicket rather than have gone over it?

If the answers to these are all 'Yes', you should be out.

If you had made no stroke at a ball and deliberately padded it away, even if it was outside the off stump when it hit you, you will be given out lbw if the umpire thinks the ball would have gone on to hit the wicket. So in this case the law is a bit tougher.

The clear things to remember in lbw decisions are that a batsman can never be given out for a ball that bounces outside the line of the leg stump, or for one that would have passed either side or over the top of the wicket. If you study the lines in the diagram and learn to see the lines of balls that are bowled, in a similar way, it will help you you learn to be able to make lbw decisions correctly, when you are umpire.

Stumped

You may be out 'stumped' if you go forward out of your ground when playing a stroke, then miss it while the wicketkeeper quickly catches the ball and knocks the bails off. If he can do this before you can get your feet back behind your crease line, or get your bat back on the ground behind the line, you will be out.

The wicketkeeper cannot take the ball in front of your wicket

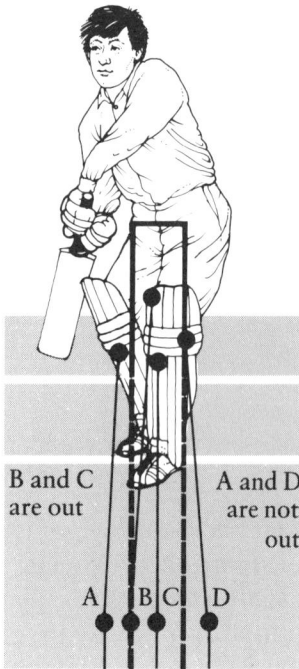

B and C
are out

A and D
are not
out

A   B C   D

when he tries to stump you, unless the ball has touched you or your bat first, and he must have the ball in the hand that breaks the wicket. But, if the ball were to hit the wicketkeeper and bounce back and hit the wicket while you were out of your ground – you would still be out stumped! Unless, of course, it was a no ball!

Run out

If your wicket is broken when you are running and are out of your ground, then you will be 'run out'. Either of the batsmen can be out this way, while the ball is in play – and remember, you can be run out from a no ball.

If the batsmen have crossed when they ran, the one running for

Out – the bat is not 'grounded'

the wicket that is broken will be out. If they have not crossed, the one who left the wicket which is broken is out. If you have stayed in your ground and the other batsman has joined you there, the other batsman will be out. In such run-outs all the runs you make will count, except for the one on which the run-out occurred.

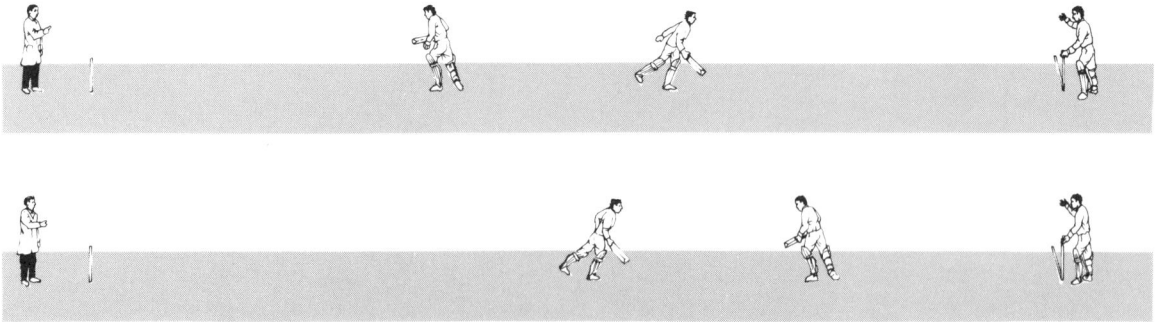

In both cases the player nearer the broken wicket is out

It is a good idea to slide the toe of your bat at full arm stretch along the ground as you near your popping crease, to remove any doubt about whether or not you make your ground.

There are four rather uncommon ways of getting out, which you should be able to avoid.

Hit ball twice

You are not allowed to hit the ball again after you have stopped it with your bat or your body. You don't get a second swing at a ball. You could be out on this law even if you just tapped a ball back to the wicketkeeper or bowler. Remember, the ball belongs to the fielding side, don't interfere with it. The only time you will be allowed to hit it again is if it looks as if it is going on to hit your wicket, when you are allowed to just prod it away with your foot or bat.

Handled ball

Never handle the ball while it is in play, unless you are specifically asked to by a fielder.

Obstructing the field

You must never deliberately get in the way of a fielder or try to hinder him when he is making a stop or a catch. The Law says you must not wilfully obstruct the opposite side by word or action!

Timed out

Make sure you are padded up and ready to bat, well before it is your turn. Wickets can fall at an alarming rate! At the start of an innings, the first four batsmen usually get ready. Be sure you have checked your place in the batting order. The captain should ensure that the ingoing batsman passes the outgoing one as he leaves the field of play. If it takes more than two minutes from the time the wicket falls, to the time the next batsman comes in, he may be given out.

Batsman retiring

You may retire at any time and resume your innings when a wicket falls, if you have the consent of the opposing captain. However, if you feel you have made enough runs and want to give someone else a chance, you may retire and end your innings and you will be considered out. *Retired, out* will be written in the score book.

Should you be hurt while batting or become too ill to continue, *retired, not out* will be entered in the score book and you may come back in later on if needed.

Runners are allowed for a batsman injured during a match who wishes to continue batting. The player acting as runner must be a member of the batting side, preferably one who has batted already. He must wear all the equipment worn by the batsman. The runner will take up position next to the square leg umpire when the injured man is receiving, and call and run with the non-striker. When the other batsman is striker, the runner takes the usual position of non-striker at the wicket and the injured man goes to square leg. If the runner is run out then the injured batsman is out. Otherwise, the injured batsman can be out in all the usual ways.

MATCHES AND RESULTS

A match may be of one or two innings for each side. The innings are always taken alternately, unless in a two-innings match the side that batted first leads by so many runs after the second side have batted that they can ask the second side to bat again immediately, or 'follow on'.

If the match is of one innings, the number of overs is sometimes limited. Matches of 20, 40 or 60 overs per side are all quite common.

Many club matches are of one innings only. The first side bat until they are all out or until they feel they have enough runs to win and so *declare* their innings finished. This declaration can be made by the captain of the batting side at any time during a match. He has to allow enough time to get all the other side's batsmen out in order to win the match, so he must balance up the number of runs he needs and the time required to get the other side out, before he makes the declaration.

Intervals

Lunch and tea may be taken during a match. In a one-day match the time for tea need not be fixed; it may be agreed to take it between innings. If bad weather or poor light interferes with play, intervals are usually brought forward. It is normal for an interval of 10 minutes to be taken between innings.

Many variations exist in matters of time, intervals and overs. The only important point is to ensure that everybody knows what the captains and umpires have agreed before the start of the game.

Getting a result

The side which scores more runs in its completed innings is the winner. A completed innings is one in which the side is all out, or has declared its innings completed. If the second side still has batsmen who have not come out to bat when play is over, they have not completed their innings and the result is a draw. If the second side scores exactly the same number of runs as the first, and the innings is completed, the game is a tie.

An 80,000 crowd watching the 4th Test between India and England in Calcutta, 1982

Therefore there are three possible results to cricket matches. A win, a draw or a tie.

In a limited-over match, however, the result can only be a win or a tie. The nature of these competitions is different. Each side sets out to score as many runs as possible in the allotted number of overs. If a side is all out before the end of their innings, they miss the chance to score runs from those overs. When both sides score exactly the same number of runs it is a tie. If the number of overs cannot be played because of bad weather or light, a result may be determined by the run rate or average number of runs per over. If the match is delayed when time is lost, the number of overs for each side is reduced.

In some one-day matches played by clubs a limit is sometimes put on the number of overs that can be taken by the first batting side, in order to ensure that the second side have a chance to get a result. This does not mean they are limited-over matches, as the second side is not restricted to any number of overs.

The result of a finished match is stated as a win by runs, if the side batting first wins. In the case of a side batting last, the result is given in the number of wickets still to fall. The example shows this.

Side A scored 176 all out; side B scored 170 all out.
Result: Side A won by 6 runs.

Side A scored 176 all out; side B scored 177 with only 8 batsmen out.
Result: Side B won by 2 wickets.

FAIR AND UNFAIR PLAY

Cricket has a tradition of fair play, in fact the words 'cricket' and 'fair play' can almost have the same meaning. There are a number of things that are considered unfair, and it should not be necessary for your captain to have to remind you of them or for the umpires to have to stop the game and bring them to your attention. They are really part of the spirit in which the game is played.

Lifting the seam or changing the condition of the ball

The ball may be polished, by any member of the fielding side, but you are not allowed to try to lift the seam of the ball, pick at it or rub any artificial substances, such as hair oil, onto the ball. You can, however, dry a wet ball or take the mud off it.

Distracting the striker

The striker should be allowed to concentrate on the ball that is being sent to him by the bowler. He should never be disturbed by noises or movements from the fielding side. It is harder to control the crowd, but experienced cricket spectators will make sure they are quiet and still during the delivery of a ball, too.

Obstructing the batsmen

When the batsmen are running, the fielders must not deliberately get in their way. If they do the umpire will signal 'dead ball' and allow the run to be completed or the boundary scored.

Bowling fast, short-pitched balls (bouncers)

These are balls bowled by a fast bowler that bounce off the pitch and fly upwards towards the top part of a batsman's body. They are considered unfair if they are used too often with the aim of frightening a batsman or causing him injury. It is not unfair to bowl bouncers – or even to bowl lots of them – at batsmen who can play them. The umpire only intervenes to caution the bowler when he feels they are being used too often in an intimidating way, or where the batsman does not have the skill to deal with them.

Trying to play a shot against a bouncer can be a risky business; Lawson (AUST) v Botham (ENG)

The bowling of fast, high, full pitches (beamers)

The bowling of beamers is considered unfair. These balls are dangerous; whizzing past the batsman quickly at head height, they could do him severe damage. The umpire will warn the bowler if he sees any of these bowled to frighten a batsman.

Time-wasting

Time-wasting is unfair because it can be used deliberately to gain an advantage. Bowlers could walk to their positions very, very slowly; fielders could cross over slowly after having their positions changed; fielders could throw the ball to one another before returning it to the bowler, who could wait before returning to his mark; the batsmen, too, could take a long time coming out and a long time looking around and taking guard. As a guide, they should always be ready to take strike when the bowler is ready to begin. These are all forms of sharp practice, which won't be tolerated by the umpires, who will realise what is going on and caution the captains.

Damage to the pitch

When a bowler bowls onto a smooth and even surface, the ball will bounce off in a fairly predictable way. However, if the pitch is

No suggestion of unfair play here, but a real mix up at an attempted run-out; the batsman was eventually not out

rough or broken up, the ball will come off in a more erratic way and so be much more difficult to hit.

A pitch can be damaged by fielders running across it, by bowlers running on it when they finish their action, or even by the batsmen themselves. Damage, once done, cannot be repaired and may result in a serious disadvantage to one side. So it is important for you to be careful of the part of the pitch which is the 'danger area'. Umpires are responsible for making sure that this area is protected and will warn any players who damage it, intentionally or otherwise.

Stealing a run

An arranged attempt by both batsmen to 'steal' a run during the bowler's run-up or delivery, is considered unfair. The bowler may

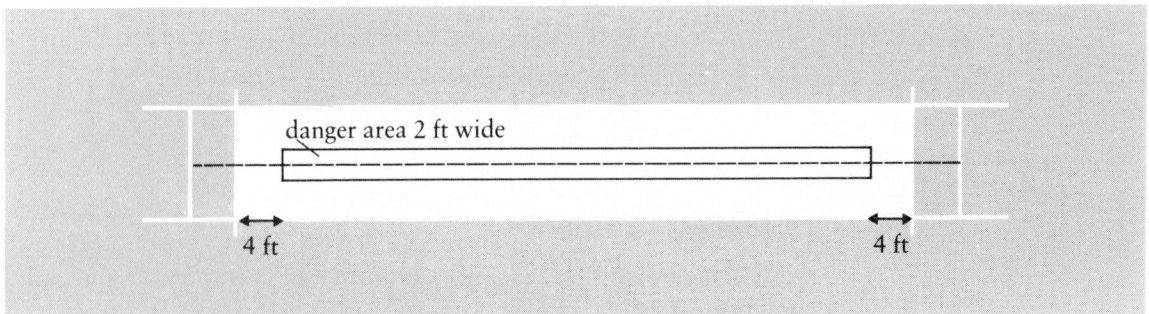

danger area 2 ft wide

4 ft

4 ft

try to run out either of the batsmen. If the bowler sees the non-striking batsman backing up for a run and out of his crease he may stop his action and run him out. However, it is customary for the bowler to just stop, demonstrate that he could run the non-striker out and so give him a warning. The bowler may then run out the non-striker if he backs up too early again.

Conduct on field

Immediate acceptance of the umpire's decision is very much a part of the game of cricket. Any criticism of the umpire by word or deed or the showing of any dissent is considered inappropriate. Traditionally, if a batsman is obviously out, he leaves the pitch or 'walks' before the umpire has even made his decision.

A strong appeal for lbw from Rodney Marsh (AUST) against Geoffrey Boycott (ENG)

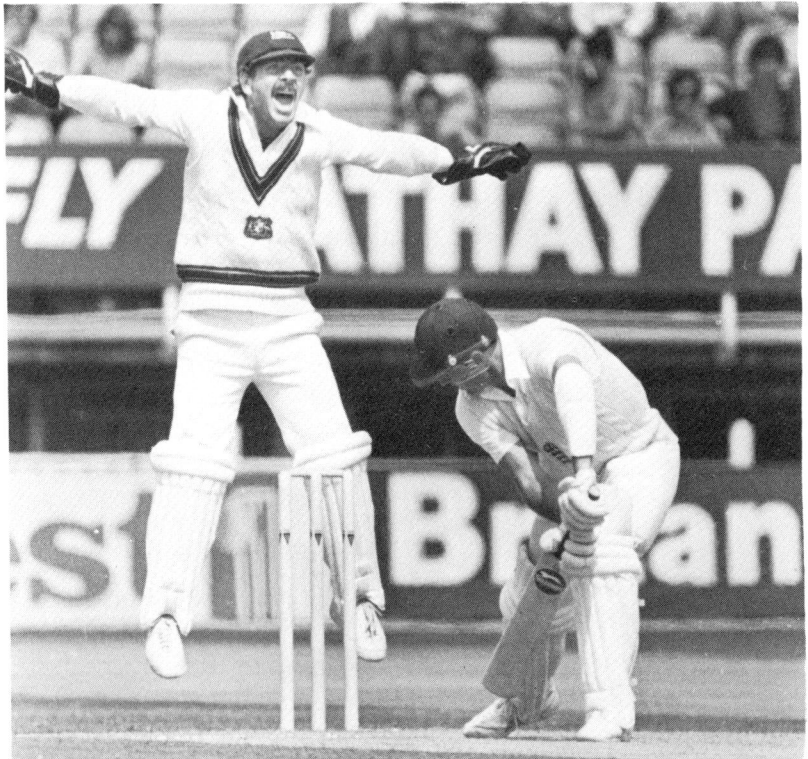

Over-appealing

The umpire can only give a batsman out if there is an appeal from the fielding side, but only the players involved in the decision need to appeal – these may be the bowler, the wicketkeeper, a fielder involved in a run-out, or one who makes a catch. If the whole side appeal with great force it puts pressure on the umpires. Loud and unnecessary appealing is considered unfair.

THE DUTIES OF THE UMPIRES

No match can be played without two umpires. They control the game. One stands at the striker's end, side-on to the wicket at the square leg position. The other stands at the bowler's end looking over the wicket down the pitch at the striker's wicket. At the end of the over, the fielders change ends, but the umpires remain at their ends for the whole innings. They just change their positions, so the square leg umpire becomes bowler's end umpire and vice versa for the next over.

The responsibilities of the umpires are
- to make decisions when asked if a batsman is out
- to signal whether a batsman is out
- to signal the score to the scorers
- to make sure that play is fair
- to call overs and intervals
- to decide about the fitness of the ground, the weather and the light.

Before a match umpires are responsible for checking the pitch and the wickets and making sure that any special conditions affecting the match are agreed beforehand. Each umpire has special duties during the match.

Bowler's end umpire

- Informs the striker of the bowler's action (i.e. which side of the stumps he will be bowling from and which arm he will use).
- Gives guard to the striker, checks sightscreen adjustments.
- Checks everyone is ready and calls 'play' at the start of an innings or after an interval.
- Counts the number of balls in an over and calls 'over'.
- Calls and signals 'no balls', 'wides', 'short runs' at his end, and signals boundaries.
- Answers appeals for 'bowled', 'caught', 'handled ball', 'hit ball twice', 'lbw', 'obstructing the field', 'timed out' and 'run out' at his end.
- Calls and signals 'dead ball' when applicable.
- Watches for pitch damage.
- Watches for unfair play.

- Indicates to scorer when one hour of play remains (where this is important).
- Calls 'time' at end of play or before intervals.

The bowler's end umpire – Swarup Kishan from India watching Derek Underwood (ENG)

Striker's end (square leg) umpire

- Counts balls in overs as a check.
- Calls and signals 'short runs' at his end.
- Answers appeals for 'hit wicket', 'stumped' and 'run out' at his end.
- Observes bowler's action for fair delivery.
- Calls and signals 'dead ball' if applicable.
- Checks number of fielders behind the popping crease at time of bowler's delivery.
- Watches for unfair play.
- Checks correctness of scores to help his colleague.

An umpire may, at any time, consult the other umpire if he is unsure of the decision he should make.

six runs

bye

one short

no ball

four runs

dead ball

out

wide

leg-bye

The umpire perfectly
positioned to see a run-out

Ground, weather and light

Umpires must judge whether the ground, weather and light are fit
for play. Poor light would give an advantage to the fielding side, as
the batsmen would find it hard to see the ball. If the ground became
wet and slippery, bowlers or fielders might injure themselves.
However, there may be occasions when a captain would rather
continue a match to its conclusion, despite a disadvantage, so before
deciding to stop play, the umpires consult both captains (the
batsmen at the wicket speak for the captain of the batting side). If
both captains wish to continue, then play goes on.

If the umpires, during play, feel the light is too poor, the batting
side have the option of continuing play. If later on the batsmen
decide to appeal against the light, the umpires will support them only
if the light has since deteriorated.

The signals

The signals are made by the umpires to the scorers and they should
be sure that the scorers have seen the signals before play continues.

THE JOB OF SCORING

Scorers are always required at games of cricket to make sure that the correct number of runs are recorded. A well-kept score book gives a lot of additional information: all the batsmen's innings, total scores, length of innings, boundaries hit and the way they were out. For the bowlers: the number of overs bowled, the number of overs with no runs scored off them (which are called 'maidens'), the

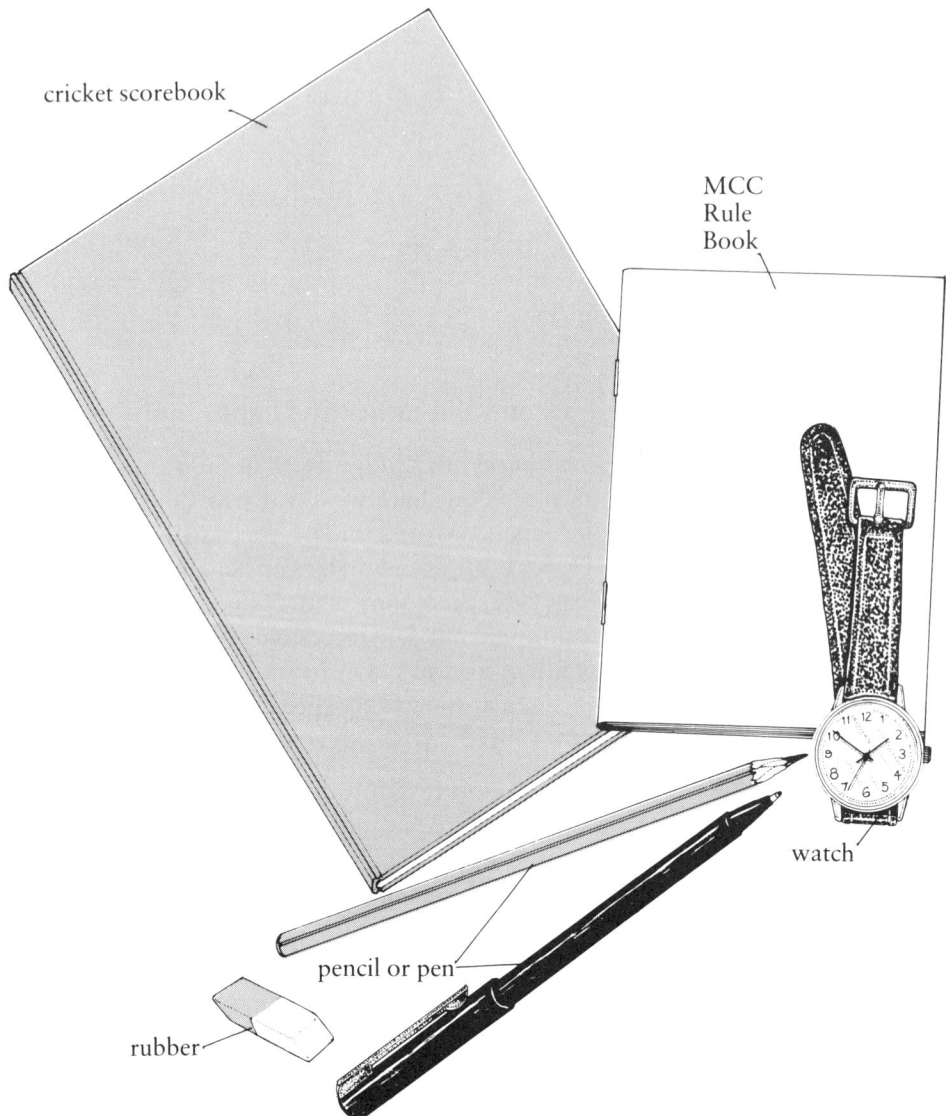

cricket scorebook

MCC
Rule
Book

watch

pencil or pen

rubber

number of wickets they took and the number of runs scored off them. In addition, the score book will show the extras awarded by the umpires.

The score book gives a fascinating record of past matches as well as your own performance over the years. The job of scoring involves concentration and accuracy as well as a detailed knowledge of the Laws. It is a good thing to learn to do, as it will develop your understanding of the game.

Usually there are two scorers – one for each side. It helps if each scorer knows the members of his own team. Scorers sit together and compare notes. It is easy enough to make mistakes when lots of

sample page from a scorebook

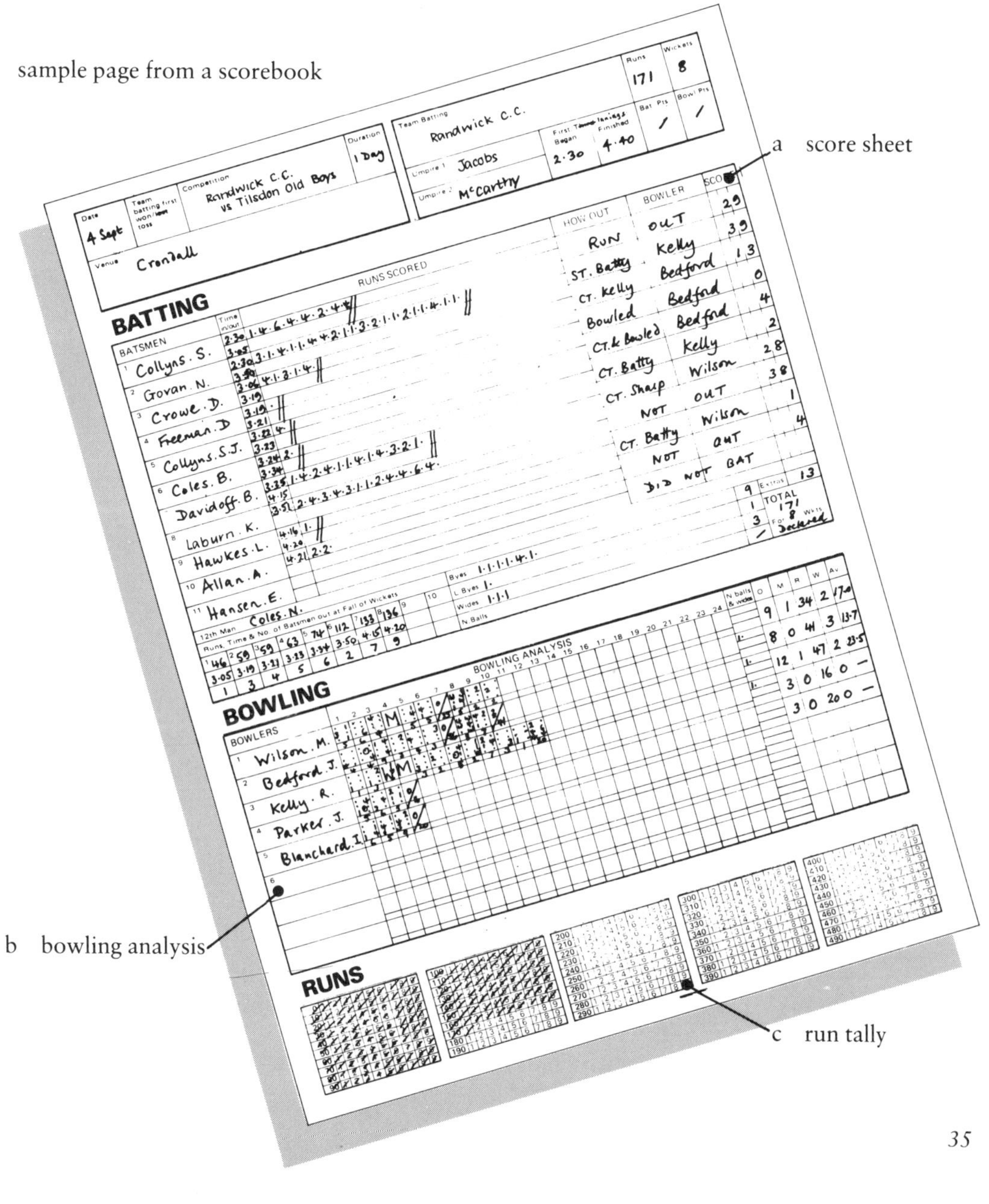

a score sheet

b bowling analysis

c run tally

things are happening and each scorer is a check on the other. Methods of scoring are a matter of routine gained from experience. As long as you stick to a familiar routine and make constant cross-checks, it should be possible to avoid bad errors.

The bowling analysis gives a check on the score sheet and records the bowling performance from which averages can be taken. Square boxes give space for each ball in the over to be recorded by a dot. If runs are scored they are entered as numbers. 'W' indicates a wicket, '+' a wide the '0' a no ball. The dots are joined up to form an 'M' for a maiden over or a 'W' for a maiden over in which the bowler took a wicket. The score book also has a list of numbers which can be crossed off to give a running total. This is a third check on accuracy.

Apart from recording the game in the book, the scorers are responsible for keeping the scoreboard up to date.

Signals of umpires

Scorers must acknowledge the umpires' signals and record the runs they signal, even if they think they know better. If five balls are bowled in an over, five balls should be recorded. If it happens a few times, draw it to the attention of the umpires at the end of an over. If you think byes have been scored, but the umpire makes no signal, score them as runs. The umpire controls the game, not the scorer.

Some important points for scorers

- If a batsman is caught out, no runs are allowed.
- If a batsman is run out, the run in question is not allowed, but the previous ones are.
- Overthrows are credited to the striker's total unless they follow the running of an extra.
- If the striker plays on, his dismissal is entered as 'bowled'.
- If the batsman is out for obstruction, the runs made before the dismissal count.
- If a fielder fields the ball with anything but his person (for example, with his hat) it counts as five runs to the striker (or extras if signalled).
- No balls not played with the bat are scored as 1 N.B. or 1, 2, or 3 if the batsmen run; 4 if the ball reaches the boundary. No balls played with the bat and no run taken, then 1 N.B. is scored. If the batsmen do run, 1, 2, or 3 are credited to the striker; if it reaches the boundary, 4 or 6 to the striker. A run of 1 cancels the 1 penalty. The penalty is never scored in addition to the runs. One more ball is bowled in the over.

- If the batsmen run 1 from a wide, it is not scored in addition. They may decide to run 1 to change ends, but this run would have been scored anyway. Wides are always extras. One more ball is bowled in the over.
- Byes are always extras and not counted as runs on the batsman's total.
- More than the boundary may be scored if the batsmen manage to run more before the ball crosses the boundary: the larger number is scored.

THE LANGUAGE OF PLAYING

Knowing the language of playing cricket is very much a part of the game. Cricketers will not only discuss the game but individual balls and the strokes played. Unless you learn what the words mean, it will be difficult to know what is being said.

The bowling

Line and length are the two most important aspects of bowling. The line is the direction of the ball after it leaves the bowler's hand. A good line is one that will hit the wicket. The *length* is the spot on the pitch where the ball bounces. A good length is not necessarily always in the same place, but depends on the speed of the ball and the condition of the pitch. If the ball has the batsman in two minds – whether to come forward to play or to go back – it is usually a good length. A ball that is *short of a length*, generally gives the batsman a chance to play a good stroke.

Good line and length are the signs of a capable bowler. The *flight* of the ball is the path it follows through the air before it bounces or *pitches* on the ground. One way of varying the flight of the ball is to use *swing*.

Both the *out-swinger* and the *in-swinger* curve in arcs towards the stumps. Look at the difference between them in the illustration.

In *spin* bowling, the ball is said to *turn*. The *off spinner* or *off break* bowler grips the ball around the seam and as he delivers the ball gives it a turn away from his body with his fingers. The ball should pitch and then turn in towards the stumps. The *leg spinner* or *leg break* bowler turns the wrist in the opposite direction and the ball spins the other way.

The speed or *pace* of the bowling can also be varied. Fast bowling obviously gives the batsmen less time to think about their shots, but the line and length of the balls are still important. Slow bowling may beat the batsman just as easily by being deceptive.

Here are some names used to describe different balls:
- *full toss* – a ball that does not *pitch* or bounce at all before it reaches the batsman

off break

point of
contact
or "pitch"

leg break

right hand bowler

right hand bowler

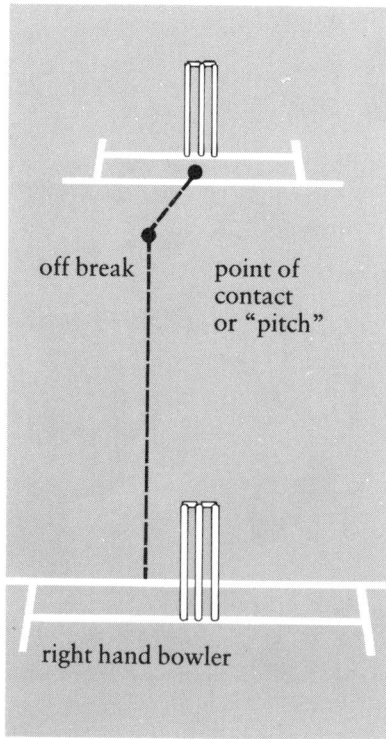

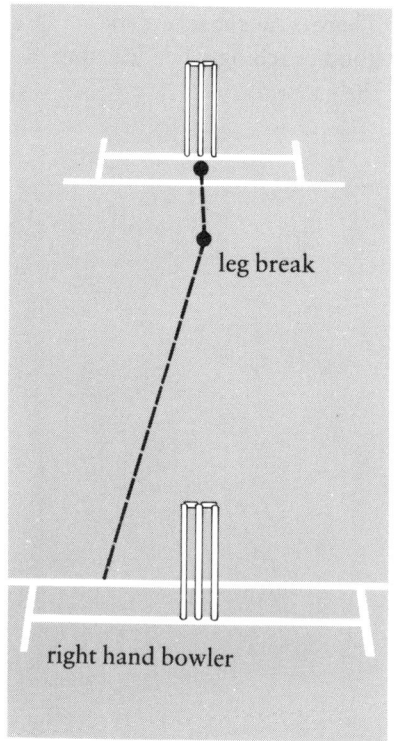

slow bowling to right hand batsman

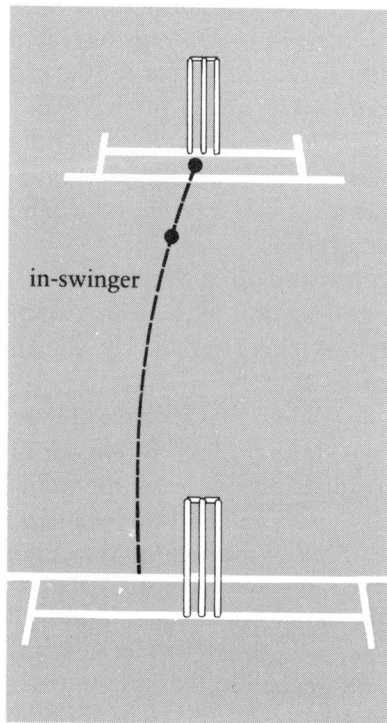

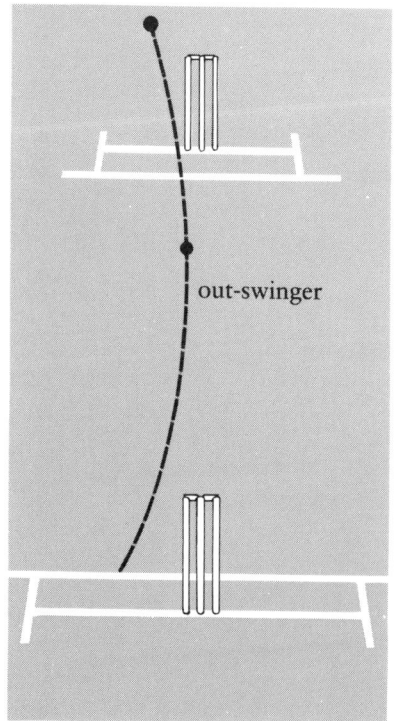

in-swinger

out-swinger

medium/fast bowling to right hand batsman

There is no substitute for good coaching when learning the game

- *yorker* – if the ball bounces right on the batsman's toes or just under his bat, it is called a yorker; getting out to one of these balls is known as being *yorked*
- *daisy cutter* or *grub* – one that pitches and then does not bounce up very high, but stays near the ground; this is a very common type of ball on grassy pitches
- *beamer* – is a ball that is a fast full toss at head height
- *bouncer* – this ball bounces off the pitch and flies up at head height; the bowler pitches the ball very short and may send it down very fast
- *leg cutter* and *off cutter* – balls that pitch on their seams and change direction, as the seam *cuts* into the pitch: a leg cutter turns into the wicket from the leg side and an off cutter turns in from the other side
- *googly* – a ball that looks as if it will be a leg break, but turns to the on side as the ball is spun out of the back of the hand in the opposite direction to the apparent movement of the wrist
- *chinaman* – a ball bowled by a left-arm bowler, spun out of the back of the hand in the opposite direction to the apparent movement of the wrist, so that it looks as if it will be an off break but it turns to the off side (leg break)
- *flipper* – a leg break bowler bowls these when he puts some top spin on the ball so that it bounces upwards rather than breaking
- *long hop* – a ball that is very short and easy to hit because it comes right on to the batsman and gives him time to find his shot and hit the ball well

- *arm ball* – can be the off spinner's ace card – this is the ball he does not turn, but sends on straight; the batsman, expecting the ball to turn, may be fooled by this one

Batting

There are two main types of batting strokes: the defensive strokes you would not expect to score from, and attacking shots which send the ball to various parts of the field so that you can run. The diagram of the field shows the scoring areas for the strokes and will make the differences between them easier to understand.

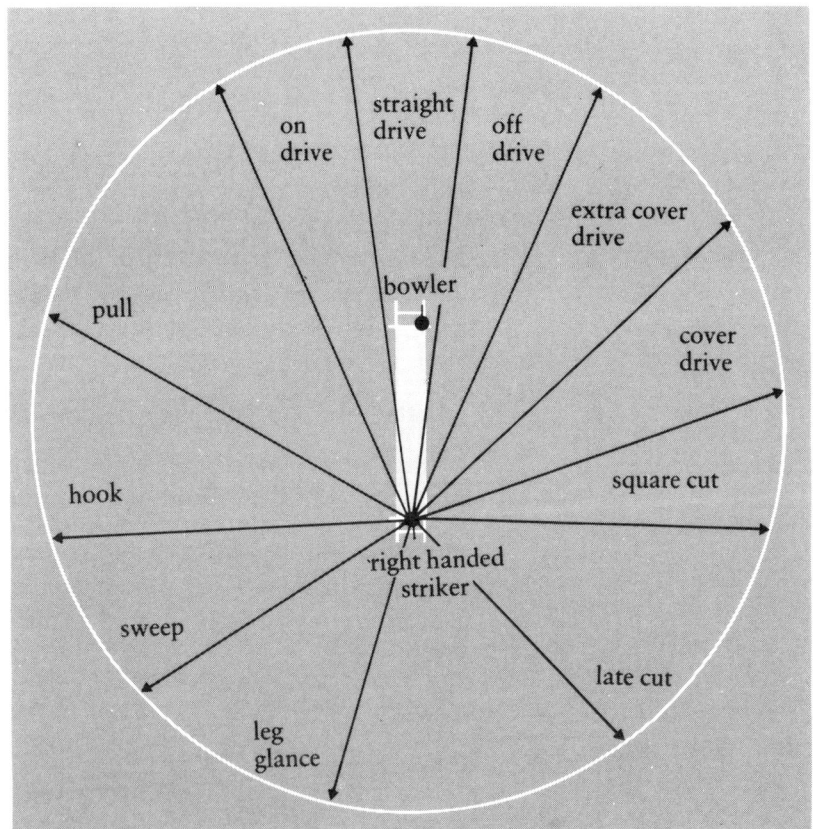

Defensive strokes: front and back foot

The *forward defensive* stroke is one of the most important in cricket. It enables you to survive against good-length, straight balls. The front foot goes forward to the pitch of the ball, the bat comes down and blocks the ball, which should travel a very short distance in front of you along the ground.

The *backward defensive* shot is also vital, particularly against fast bowling. The feet move backwards and the weight of the body is transferred to the back foot. Elbows are kept high and the batsman just lets the ball come on to the bat, so that it then drops to the ground close in front of him.

All defensive shots are played without a follow-through and with a minimum of backlift and power.

Drives

The drive starts with a high backlift as you pick up the line of the ball, then you put your front foot and weight out to it, swing down with a straight bat and through the ball into a follow-through.

The *off drive* can be played to a ball that is a good length and in a line with, or outside the off stump. The *on drive* is the same stroke, but squarer to the line of the ball, and is played to a ball pitching on or outside the leg stump.

The *straight drive* and the *cover drive* are the other main ones, the former going past the bowler and the latter going between extra cover and cover. Drives are usually hit along the ground but you can play a *lofted drive* which has an exaggerated uplift and follow-through which can send the ball for six.

Cuts

Cuts can be played against any delivery short and wide of the off stump, especially one bowled by a fast bowler.

The *square cut* involves hitting the ball away from a standing position. The *late cut* is a refinement of the square cut, which aims at steering the ball just behind the stumps on the off side.

Pull and hook

The *pull* and the *hook* are played against any short delivery coming right at your body or on a line with the stumps. It's very exciting to watch someone hooking bouncers casually away to square leg; but it takes a lot of practice to do this.

Sweep

The *sweep* is used when the ball pitches outside the leg stump. It is often a good weapon against spin bowling.

Glance

The *glance* is a little deflection of the ball down the leg side.

TEST YOUR KNOWLEDGE

1   In what year were the first recorded laws of cricket drawn up?

2   The batsman hits the ball in the air to the boundary. A fielder catches the ball inside the field of play but has one foot over the boundary rope or line. What is the umpire's reply to an appeal for 'caught'?

3   The batsman mis-hits the ball and sees it rolling towards his wicket. He knocks it away with his bat. Is this fair play?

4   There are eleven ways a batsman can get out. What are they?

5   In your view what should the umpire give for the following appeals for lbw from a right-arm bowler going over the wicket to a right-handed batsman when

    (a) the ball pitches outside leg stump and hits the back pad below the knee directly in front of the wicket?

    (b) a good-length ball pitches on line between the wickets and strikes the batsman's front pad in front of the stumps?

    (c) the batsman receives the same ball as in (b) above but it snicks his bat before hitting the pad?

    (d) the batsman receives the same ball as in (b) above but it snicks his bat after hitting the pad?

    (e) the batsman plays and misses a ball pitching outside the line of the off stump which hits his pads, also outside the line of off stump, but would have gone on to hit the wicket?

    (f) the batsman receives the same ball as in (e) above but does not attempt to play a stroke and is hit on his pad in the same way?

6   Imagine you are batting and standing at the non-striker's end and your partner hits the ball to fine leg. Who should normally call for the run?

7   You set off for a run but your batting partner decides to stay in his crease. Nevertheless, you carry on until you're occupying his crease too! The ball is returned to the other end and the wicket broken. Which of you is out?

8   The batsman edges a rising ball to the wicketkeeper, who makes a fair catch. Nobody appeals and the batsman stays in his ground. What happens next?

9   One of your braver team mates is fielding at forward short leg and wearing a protective helmet. The batsman middles a pull shot which hits the fielder's helmet and is then caught by the

bowler, who appeals. What is the umpire's decision?

10 The batsmen complete five runs before the ball trickles over the boundary by the long-on fielder. How many runs do they score?

11 The batsmen complete a sharp single but the fielder's throw misses the stumps and reaches the boundary on the other side. How many runs do they score?

12 The umpire calls 'no ball' and the batsman pushes the ball wide and takes an easy single. What is the entry in the score book?

13 In a limited-over game what are the possible results (weather permitting!)?

14 Which captain usually spins the coin to decide who elects to bat or bowl first?

15 What is the aim of declaring an innings closed before it is completed?

16 A bowler decides to switch from over the wicket to round the wicket. What must he do first?

17 You've been injured while batting and call for a runner:
    (a) Where should you stand when your batting partner is receiving?
    (b) Who calls for a run when you are at the receiving end and play the ball in front of the wicket?

18 At the end of a normal single-innings game the scores are: Team A, 180–6 declared; Team B, 181–7. What is the result?

19 At the end of a limited-over single-innings game the scores are: Team A, 200 all out; Team B, 192–1. What is the result?

20 In your view the umpire has made a serious error in not giving an opposing batsman 'out' when he was clearly caught behind the wicket. What do you do?

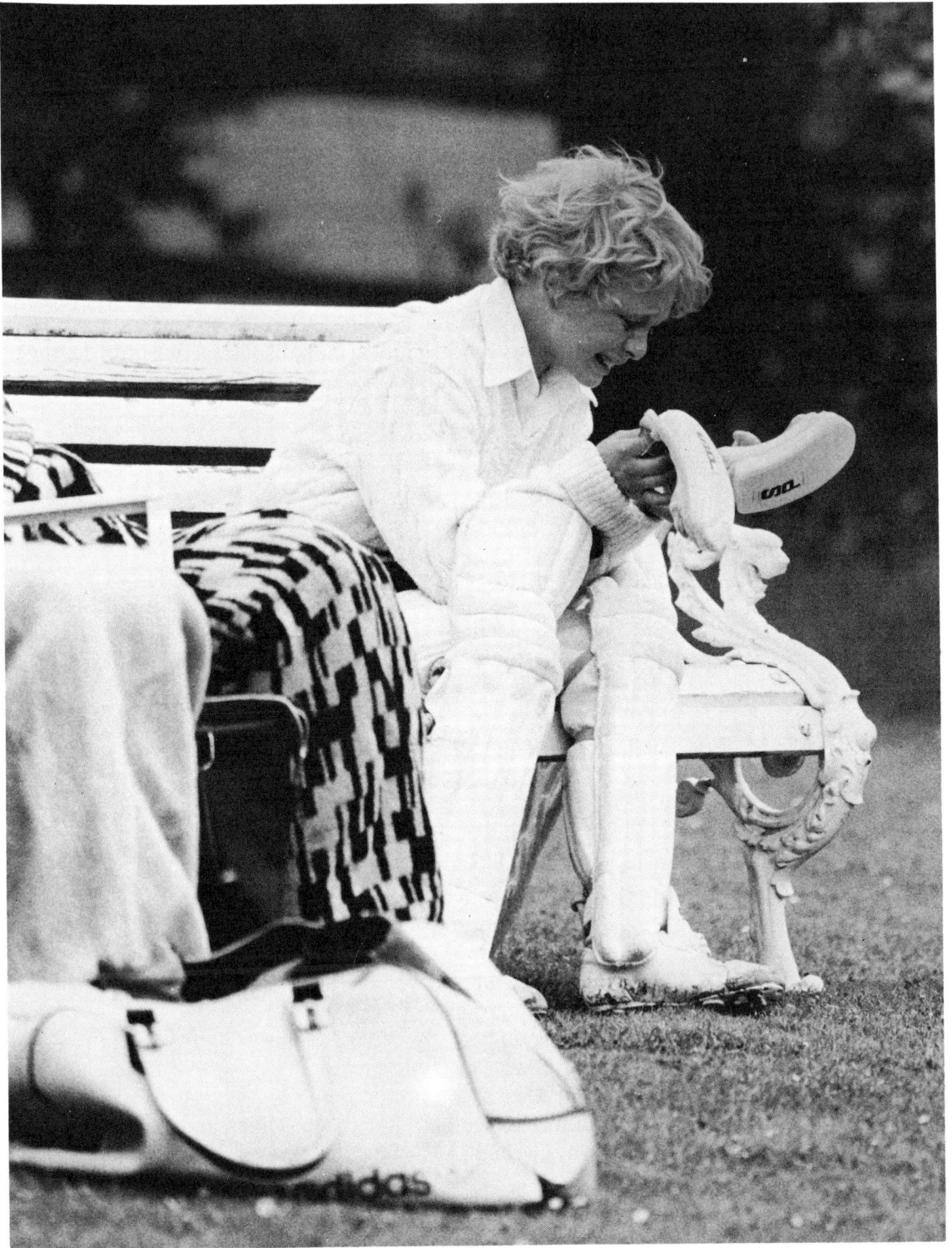

Cricket can be a cruel game. Out first ball!

ANSWERS

1   1744.

2   'Not out' and a signal of six runs to the striker.

3   Yes.

4   Bowled; hit wicket; caught; leg before wicket; stumped; run out; hit ball twice; handled the ball; obstructing the field; timed out; retired out.

5   (a) 'Not out'.
     (b) 'Out'.
     (c) 'Not out'.
     (d) 'Out'.
     (e) 'Not out'.
     (f) 'Out'.

6   You should.

7   You are.

8   Play resumes with the next delivery.

9   'Not out'.

10   Five.

11   Five.

12   One run to the striking batsman's total.
     One run to the total score and one with a circle round it in the bowler's analysis. No extras. Note also that an extra ball must be bowled.

13   Win or tie.

14   The home team captain.

15   To give the batting side plenty of time to get the fielding side all out and so win.

16   Inform the umpire who, in turn, will inform the batsman.

17   (a) At square leg.
     (b) The runner.

18   Team B wins by 3 wickets.

19   Team A wins by 8 runs.

20   Nothing. The umpire's decision is final, and to show dissent is always wrong and against the spirit of the game.

The M.C.C. have kindly granted the Publishers permission to reproduce, in this book, a simplified version of the Laws of Cricket for the purposes of introducing young players to the game. However it is important to have a copy of the full Laws and Notes. Copies of the current edition of the official Laws of Cricket with full Notes and Interpretations in English can be obtained from Lord's Cricket Ground, price £0.70 including postage.

ACKNOWLEDGEMENTS

We should like to thank the following for permission to reproduce their photographs;
All-Sport/Adrian Murrell; pages 3, 11, 13 right, 25, 27, 28, 45
Colorsport; cover and pages 15, 29, 40
Patrick Eagar; pages 5, 13 left, 19, 31, 33
Supersport; page 1
The line illustrations are by Nick May.

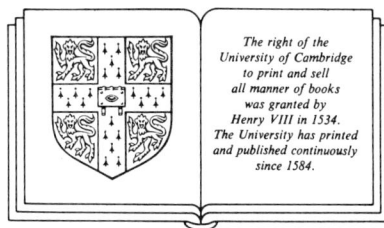

The right of the
University of Cambridge
to print and sell
all manner of books
was granted by
Henry VIII in 1534.
The University has printed
and published continuously
since 1584.

Published by the Press Syndicate of the University of Cambridge
The Pitt Building, Trumpington Street, Cambridge CB2 1RP
32 East 57th Street, New York, NY 10022, USA
10 Stamford Road, Oakleigh, Melbourne 3166, Australia

© Cambridge University Press 1984

First published 1984
Fourth printing 1989

Printed in Great Britain at the University Press, Cambridge

British Library cataloguing in publication data
Freeman, Gill
Cricket. – (Sportmaster)
1. Cricket
I.Title   II. Series
796.35'82   GV917
ISBN 0 521 27533 4
MX